Eyes on the Sky

Asteroids

by Don Nardo

KIDHAVEN PRESS

THOMSON

GALE

Detroit • New York • San Diego • San Francisco
Boston • New Haven, Conn. • Waterville, Maine
London • Munich

Library of Congress Cataloging-in-Publication Data

Nardo, Don, 1947–
  Asteroids / by Don Nardo.
    p. cm.—(Eyes on the sky)
Includes bibliographical references.
Summary: Discusses the discovery of asteroids, the various types, their possible uses, and the ultimate threat of an asteroid impact with the Earth.
  ISBN 0-7377-0998-7 (hardback : alk. paper)
1. Asteroids—Juvenile literature. [1. Asteroids.] I. Title. II. Series.
  QB651 .N37   2002
  523 .44—dc21

2001004961

Picture Credits

On Cover: © Roger Ressmeyer/CORBIS
© AFP/CORBIS, 24
Associated Press, 41
© Julian Baum/SPL/Photo Researchers, Inc., 20
© Jonathan Blair/CORBIS, 36
© CORBIS, 19, 30, 32
© Frank Lane Picture Agency/CORBIS, 28
© Mark Garlick/SPL/Photo Researchers, Inc., 11
© Getty Images, 18
© Giraudon/Art Resource, NY, 9
© A. Gragera, Latin Stock/SPL/Photo Researchers, Inc., 26
© David A. Hardy/SPL/Photo Researchers, Inc., 37 (top)
Chris Jouan and Martha Schierholz, 5
JPL, 38
© Claus Lunau/Bonnier Publications/SPL/Photo Researchers, Inc., 37 (bottom)
© NASA/Roger Ressmeyer/CORBIS, 35
Brandy Noon, 6–7, 13, 14, 22
© Detlev Van Ravenswaay/SPL/Photo Researchers, Inc., 16
© Roger Ressmeyer/CORBIS, 40
© Stapleton Collection/CORBIS, 8

Copyright 2002 by KidHaven Press,
an imprint of The Gale Group
10911 Technology Place, San Diego, CA 92127

Printed in the U.S.A.

Table of Contents

1
Asteroids and Their Origins

An **asteroid** is a small rocky or metallic object that **orbits,** or moves around, the sun. **Planets**—such as Earth, Mars, Jupiter, and Saturn—move around the sun, too. But asteroids are much smaller than planets. In fact, the largest known asteroid, Ceres, is many times smaller than the smallest planet, Mercury. For this reason, astronomers (scientists who study the stars, planets, and other heavenly bodies) sometimes call asteroids "minor planets."

The Missing Planet

Despite their small size, the discovery of asteroids was big news for science. Before this discovery, astronomers thought that the **solar system** contained only a few objects. (The solar system is made up of the sun and all of the objects that orbit it.) In 1781, William Herschel, an English astronomer, discovered the planet Uranus. That brought the number of known planets to seven, the other six being Mercury, Venus, Earth, Mars, Jupiter, and Saturn.

But most astronomers were not satisfied. They suspected that at least one more planet was lurking in the dark depths of space. The reason for this suspicion was the way the known planets were spaced. Starting with Mercury, the closest to the sun, each successive planet was about twice as far from the sun as the one before it. So the distances of the planets formed a rough mathematical pattern. This pattern became known as **Bode's Law**, after

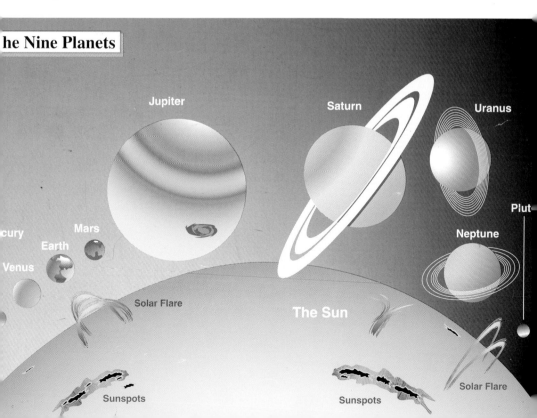

he Nine Planets

Jupiter

Saturn

Uranus

Plut

cury

Mars

Neptune

Earth

Venus

Solar Flare

The Sun

Sunspots

Sunspots

Solar Flare

Actual Distance

Pluto		Neptune		Uranus		Saturn		Jupiter		Mars		Earth		Venus		Mercury		Sun
39.3		30.06		19.18		9.55		5.2		1.52		1.		.72		.39		

Johann Bode, the German astronomer who recognized it.

The trouble was that Bode's Law was like a puzzle with a missing piece. All seven of the known planets followed the pattern fairly well, but the law also predicted that an eighth planet should exist between the orbits of Mars and Jupiter. No such planet had ever been seen. Yet most astronomers came to believe that it must exist.

In 1800, a group of noted German astronomers met and agreed to conduct a search for the missing planet. Each of these scientists had access to a powerful telescope. With so many telescopes devoted to the search, the members of the group were confident that they would be suc-

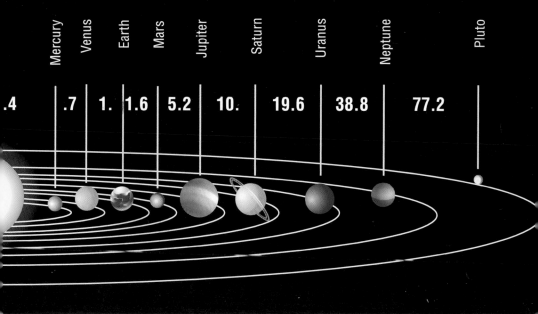

Bode's Prediction

Mercury	Venus	Earth	Mars	Jupiter	Saturn	Uranus	Neptune	Pluto
.4	.7	1.	1.6	5.2	10.	19.6	38.8	77.2

cessful. They soon became known in the popular press as the "sky police."

The Discovery of Ceres

However, before the so-called sky police had a chance to begin their search, another astronomer beat them to the punch. On January 1, 1801, the first day of the nineteenth century, an Italian named Giuseppe Piazzi peered through his own telescope at a section of the constellation Taurus, the bull. Piazzi observed the stars through his lens. Then he looked at a standard star chart of the constellation that showed all the known stars in Taurus. Something was clearly odd, Piazzi realized: One of the stars he saw through the lens was not on the chart.

An artist's view of the mythical bull outlined by the stars of the constellation Taurus.

Piazzi immediately suspected that the unidentified object might be the missing planet needed to fill the gap in Bode's Law. To make sure the object was moving, as planets do, he observed it the following night. Sure enough, it had shifted its position in relation to the fixed background stars. Between January 3 and February 11, Piazzi made twenty more observations of the mysterious object before it moved behind the sun.

Piazzi notified other astronomers about his discovery. And after the object reappeared from the sun's glare several months later, other observers confirmed its existence. Piazzi named the object Ceres, after an ancient Roman goddess of agriculture. That same year, a German mathematician, Karl F. Gauss, calculated Ceres' orbit. Gauss found that the object lay between Mars and Jupiter, right where Bode's Law predicted that a planet should exist. So quite naturally, he, Piazzi, and most other astronomers

A painting of the Roman goddess Ceres, after whom the first known asteroid was named.

assumed that Ceres was the missing eighth planet.

A Whole New Class of Objects

It was not long, however, before scientists realized that Ceres was not a full-fledged planet. First, William Herschel calculated the object's size. He found that it was many times smaller than Mercury, the smallest known planet. Astronomers were puzzled that Ceres was so much smaller than the other planets. Then, various observers began finding other objects similar to Ceres. German astronomer Wilhelm M. Olbers discovered Pallas on March 28, 1802; another German, Karl Harding, found Juno on September 1, 1804; and Olbers located Vesta on March 29, 1807.

Calculations quickly showed that all of these new objects lay between Mars and Jupiter, just as Ceres did. The obvious question was why several minor planets orbited the sun in the region where there should have been a single major planet. Olbers may have been the first to suggest a likely explanation. Perhaps such a major planet had once existed, he said, and for reasons unknown, that body had exploded, producing several smaller fragments.

William Herschel devised a collective name for these fragments—asteroids, meaning "starlike objects." This came from the fact that even through a telescope they looked like stars. However, stars are sunlike objects lying far beyond the solar system. Astronomers had established that the asteroids were a whole new class of objects in the sun's own family.

The size of that family continued to grow as more and more asteroids were discovered in the years that followed. By 1852, twenty-three asteroids were known; by 1868, that number had risen to an even one hundred; and by 1890, astronomers had found more than three hundred asteroids. All of these, like the first four asteroids discovered, orbited between Mars and Jupiter. As a result, scientists came to call the band of space between those two planets the "**asteroid belt**."

Swarms of asteroids orbit in the region lying between Mars and Jupiter.

A New Theory for Asteroid Origins

The year 1890 marked the end of the "visual" era of asteroid discovery. Up till that time, astronomers had spotted new asteroids the way Piazzi had—by repeatedly looking back and forth from a telescope lens to a star chart. In 1891, however, German astronomer Max Wolf introduced a new, much more effective technique—photography. Wolf mounted a camera on his telescope. Then he placed a photographic plate inside the camera. The light from stars and asteroids passed through the lens and fell on the plate, which Wolf left in place for several hours. Because the stars appeared to remain stationary in the sky, their light created round dots on the plate. But the asteroids moved across the starry background, so their images left long trails on the plate. Using this method, Wolf found 232 asteroids before his death in 1932. His assistant, Karl Reinmuth, outdid him, discovering 284.

Thanks to photography, by the close of the twentieth century, many thousands of asteroids had been found. Astronomers are certain that these objects actually number in the hundreds of thousands or even millions. Most, however, are much too small to see, even in large telescopes.

The twentieth century not only revealed the existence of numerous new asteroids. Astronomers also revised their ideas about the origins of these objects. In particular, they laid to rest the theory that the asteroids formed from the explosion of an ancient planet. They showed that all of the known asteroids combined weigh less than one-thousandth as much as Earth. This is far too small to have once been a planet.

Scientists now believe that the planets formed from millions of small objects called **planetesimals**. These orbited the sun when

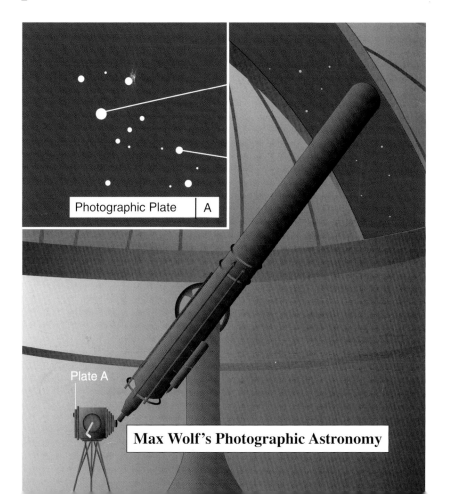

Photographic Plate | A

Plate A

Max Wolf's Photographic Astronomy

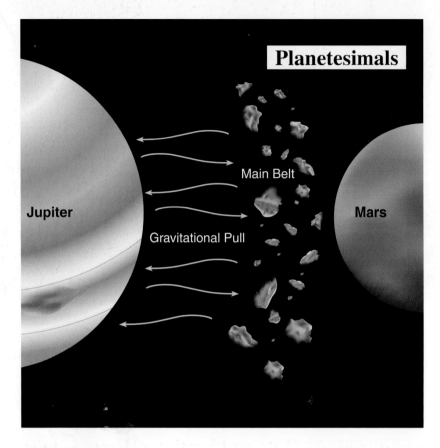

Planetesimals

Jupiter

Main Belt

Gravitational Pull

Mars

the solar system was young. **Gravity** made the planetesimals combine into larger clumps. The largest clumps of all became the planets. The exception was the swarm of planetesimals lying near Jupiter, the largest planet in the solar system. Jupiter's powerful gravity constantly pulled and pushed on these objects, keeping them from combining into a single large mass. In the end, Bode's Law turned out to be correct, except that in the region where a planet should have formed, the asteroids orbit instead.

2
Kinds of Asteroids

Astronomers need not fear being bored when studying asteroids. The fact is that no two of these objects are ever alike. Like the planets, asteroids vary greatly in size and composition. But, unlike the planets, asteroids have many different and exotic shapes, and they sometimes orbit the sun in odd ways.

Asteroid Sizes

It is not surprising that Ceres was the first asteroid to be discovered. With a diameter of about 567 miles (914 kilometers), Ceres is the largest of all the minor planets in the solar system. If one could place Ceres on Earth's surface, it would roughly cover the state of Texas.

A sketch illustrates how much asteroids can vary in size and shape.

In fact, by itself Ceres makes up about 25 percent of the **mass** (total amount of matter) of all the known asteroids. (Still, it would take more than four thousand objects the size of Ceres to equal the mass of Earth.)

Though no other asteroid compares in size with Ceres, twenty-six asteroids are larger than

124 miles (200 km) in diameter. This may not seem large when set beside Earth and other planets. But it is very large by human standards. Take Pallas, for example. The second asteroid to be found, Pallas is also the second largest, with a diameter of about 324 miles (522 km). If placed on Earth's surface, Pallas would cover the state of Pennsylvania and then some. Vesta, the next largest asteroid, is about 310 miles (500 km) in diameter, followed by Hygiea, at 275 miles (443 km); Davida, at 208 miles (336 km); and Interamnia, at 207 miles (334 km).

Astronomers are confident that they have discovered the vast majority of these and the other very large asteroids. It is estimated that about 99 percent of all asteroids larger than 62 miles (100 km) in diameter have been spotted and cataloged. However, smaller asteroids are harder to find. Of those between 6 and 62 miles in diameter, scientists estimate that only about half have been discovered. And of those a mile or less across, at least several hundred thousand remain to be found.

Asteroid Shapes

The size of an asteroid has a direct bearing on its shape. The largest asteroids—Ceres, Pallas, and Vesta—are probably **spherical** (round), like

The asteroid in the foreground is irregular because its gravity is too weak to crush it into a sphere.

the moon and Earth. This is because each of these asteroids contains enough mass for its gravity to crush its material into a ball. However, the smaller asteroids are irregular in shape. To begin with, their gravities are not strong enough to crush their materials into spheres. They have also undergone random collisions with one another over the ages. Such crashes have left their surfaces fractured, pitted, and uneven.

Typical of such uneven asteroids is Gaspara. The *Galileo* spacecraft, launched by the National Aeronautics and Space Administration (NASA), flew by Gaspara in October 1991. The spacecraft's onboard cameras snapped photos at a distance of sixteen thousand miles. These pictures revealed a potato-shaped object, roughly 12.4 by 7.4 miles, covered by **impact craters**.

Some asteroids have much more bizarre and unexpected shapes than Gaspara does. A good example is Toutatis, which looks like a dumbbell. Toutatis consists of two separate chunks—one about 2.5 miles across, the other about 1.6 miles across—that touch each other in the middle. Many experts think that the two chunks were once separate asteroids. Their mutual gravities pulled them together, but not violently enough to break them up. Instead, they gently collided and stuck to each other, and now they hurtle through the heavens together in their weird embrace. Such dumbbell-shaped asteroids are called **compound asteroids**.

The Materials Making Up Asteroids

Because asteroids vary so much in size and shape, astronomers find it too difficult to classify

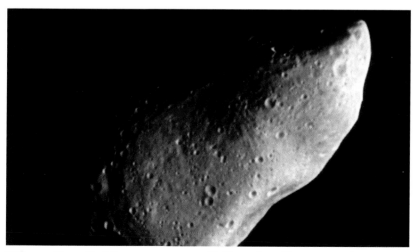

When the Galileo spacecraft flew by Gaspara in October 1991, it snapped a photo of the asteroid.

Some asteroids are dumbell-shaped, with two separate pieces held together by gravity.

them by these factors. Instead, they group these minor planets according to their composition— that is, the kinds of materials they are made of. The three main kinds of asteroid materials are known as C-type, S-type, and M-type. About 75 percent of all asteroids are C-type. They are composed of carbonlike minerals, and because carbon is usually black, they are very dark. They are so dark, in fact, that they absorb most of the light that hits them. Scientists estimate that only about 5 percent of the sunlight that reaches the surface of the average C-type aster-oid bounces back into space. For this reason, C-type asteroids are harder to see through telescopes than other kinds of asteroids. (Ceres is an exception; although it is a C-type asteroid, its unusually large size makes it fairly easy to see.)

In contrast, S-type and M-type asteroids reflect a good deal more light. Therefore, they are easier to spot. S-type asteroids are composed of a mixture of various kinds of rock and metal. Juno, the third asteroid to be discovered, is an S-type. M-types, the rarest of the three kinds of asteroid, are made up almost entirely of the metals nickel and iron. The largest known M-type is Psyche. Essentially, Psyche is a giant hunk of metal about 163 miles (264 km) across.

Asteroids with Unusual Orbits

Astronomers also categorize asteroids by the way they orbit the sun and their position in the solar system. The vast majority of these bodies lie in the asteroid belt between Mars and Jupiter. Experts often refer to these asteroids as "main belt" asteroids. Ceres, Pallas, Vesta, Hygiea, and most of the other exceptionally large minor planets are main belt asteroids.

However, a few small groups of asteroids exist outside the asteroid belt. Two of these groups are located near Jupiter. One is *pushed* by the giant planet's gravity and travels around the sun always staying a little ahead of Jupiter; the other

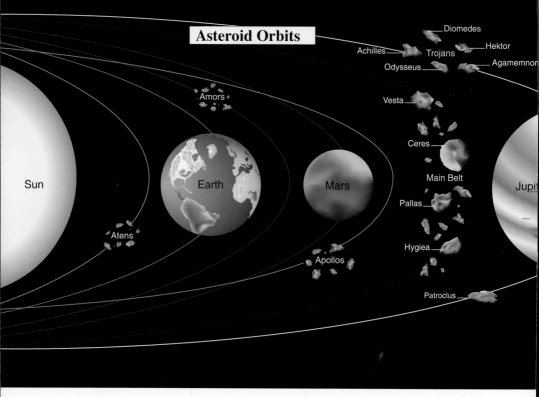

Asteroid Orbits

Sun · Atens · Apollos · Earth · Amors · Mars · Vesta · Ceres · Pallas · Hygiea · Main Belt · Patroclus · Odysseus · Achilles · Trojans · Diomedes · Hektor · Agamemnon · Jupiter

group is *pulled* by Jupiter's gravity and orbits a short distance behind the planet. Astronomers call these asteroids the Trojans. Each is named after a hero of the Trojan War, the mythical conflict in which the ancient Greeks sacked the city of Troy. Among the largest Trojans are Agamemnon, Patroclus, Diomedes, Achilles, and Odysseus. The largest of all is Hektor, at 93 miles (150 km) by 186 miles (300 km). Some scientists think that Hektor may be a dumbbell-shaped asteroid like Toutatis.

Another category of asteroids lying outside the asteroid belt are called near-Earth asteroids, or NEAs. The NEAs fall into three main groups: the Amors, Apollos, and Atens. The

Amors cross over Mars's orbit and come close to (but do not cross) Earth's orbit. Astronomers estimate that between one thousand and two thousand Amors larger than 0.6 miles (1 km) across may exist. The second group of NEAs, the Apollos, swing in from Mars's orbit and actually cross over Earth's orbit. The estimated number of Apollos larger than 0.6 miles across is between four hundred and one thousand. Finally, the Atens are asteroids that orbit mainly inside Earth's orbit, that is, closer to the sun than Earth. About a dozen or so Atens larger than 0.6 miles in diameter may exist.

Asteroids with Their Own Moons

The Trojans, Amors, Apollos, and Atens do not exist outside of the asteroid belt merely by chance. The gravities of Jupiter, Mars, Earth, and other planets push or pull these objects into their unusual paths. Not surprisingly, on occasion one of these planets actually captures an asteroid. Most astronomers think that Mars's two small moons—Deimos and Phobos—are captured asteroids. And many of Jupiter's moons are undoubtedly asteroids that strayed too close to that planet's huge gravity.

When it comes to having moons, however, the planets are not unique. In recent years,

Ida and its tiny satellite, Dactyl (at far right), as photographed by *Galileo* in 1993.

astronomers confirmed that some asteroids have moons of their own. In 1993, the *Galileo* spacecraft flew near the asteroid Ida and saw a tiny satellite-asteroid orbiting it. NASA scientists dubbed the little moon Dactyl. In 1999, a ground-based telescope discovered a moon orbiting the asteroid Eugenia. The moon is 8 miles (13 km) across, compared to Eugenia's diameter of 133 miles (214 km); the moon orbits its parent once every five days. The discovery of asteroids with their own moons is an exciting new development. It shows that the solar system is made up of dozens, and perhaps hundreds, of similar but smaller planetary and asteroidal systems.

3
Mining the Asteroids

Asteroids are not only interesting objects to view and study, but also valuable resources waiting to be exploited. At least seventy years ago, science fiction writers began depicting humans mining the asteroids. And in the 1970s, NASA scientists began discussing this idea for real.

Space Mining

Asteroids are rich in various minerals, metals, and other materials. Mining these materials would conserve supplies on Earth, which are rapidly dwindling. Also, **processing** minerals and metals (separating them from rocks and dirt) pollutes Earth's air, soil, and water. In the case of asteroid mining, this problem would be

Space explorers begin mining an asteroid's surface in this fanciful view.

eliminated because the processing would take place in space.

An obvious question is why not mine the moon first? After all, the moon is much bigger than any asteroid, and it is also much closer to Earth than the asteroids are. Most people are surprised to learn that mining the moon would be *more* costly than mining asteroids. The moon's surface gravity is about one-sixth that of Earth's. So it would take a considerable amount of fuel to land miners and their equipment on its surface. It would take even more fuel to get the processed minerals and metals off the moon's surface for shipment back to Earth.

Why Mine Asteroids?

By contrast, most asteroids are small and have extremely tiny gravities. A mining ship would not have to waste precious fuel landing. Instead, it would park beside the asteroid. An asteroid half a mile across has gravity only about one-twenty-eight thousandth that of Earth, so a miner would weigh no more than a ballpoint pen. The mined minerals would also be nearly weightless. Therefore, getting the miners and their cargo off the asteroid would require little or no fuel.

Another reason for mining asteroids rather than the moon is the purity of the materials. Take the case of valuable metals such as iron and nickel. These metals are not very plentiful on the moon's surface. And what little can be found is bound up inside rocks. It would take a great deal of time, effort, and money to separate the metals from the rocks. On S-type and especially M-type asteroids, however, the desired metals exist in large quantities. They are almost pure, so they would require very little processing. For all of these reasons, mining asteroids would be relatively cheap.

The materials mined from asteroids would be extremely valuable to people on Earth. A number of scientists have estimated what a typical asteroid mining operation might be worth. The value of such an operation would depend on the object's size. An asteroid just one hundred yards wide—the length of a football field—contains about 3 million tons of material. An operation lasting only a few weeks could extract up to ten thousand tons of this

Some asteroids contain deposits of almost pure iron like the sample seen here.

material. That is about four hundred times more than the cargo bay of a NASA space shuttle holds. So, one football field–sized asteroid could keep a mining crew busy for twenty or thirty years.

What Is an Asteroid Worth?

It is more likely, though, that scientists and space miners will go after somewhat larger asteroids, those in the range of 0.6 miles (1 km) across. Such an object has several billion tons of material. If it is an S-type asteroid, about 10 to 15 percent of this total will be a mixture of nickel and iron. That alone would be worth at least $500 billion (enough to pay each man, woman, and child in the United States $178,000). The same asteroid would also have supplies of precious metals such as platinum and gold. In addition, it would contain large amounts of sulfur, aluminum oxide, and other useful minerals. Together, the materials mined from this single small asteroid would be worth several trillion dollars. And even if teams of miners worked 365 days a year, it would take more than a century to dismantle the object.

An M-type asteroid would have even more abundant deposits of valuable metals than an S-type. However, it is more likely that at least the first several asteroids mined will be S-type or C-type. Though these kinds of asteroids have smaller amounts of metals, they have larger supplies of oxygen, hydrogen, and water. (The water is frozen rather than in liquid form, but it can be easily melted.) These materials are essential for maintaining a small colony for the miners to live in during their stay. The water can be used for drinking, cooking, and bathing, of course. Along with ordinary dirt, the oxygen, hydrogen, and some other elements can be combined in various ways to make beams, walls, pipes, and other parts of a habitat. The oxygen and hydrogen can also be used to make rocket fuel. So, relatively little fuel would have to be brought from Earth.

Mission to an NEA

NASA and some private companies have already begun drawing up plans for such mining missions. The plans call for exploiting NEAs, since these asteroids pass fairly close to Earth. (It would take much longer to get to the asteroid belt and back, and that would cost a good deal more.) Scientists have already demonstrated that they can successfully guide spacecraft to NEAs. In June 1997, NASA's *NEAR Shoemaker* spacecraft flew by and photographed asteroid 253 Mathilde, and on February 12, 2001, it reached and touched down on 433 Eros.

Unlike *NEAR Shoemaker*, mining ships will not land on asteroids. Instead, mining ships will float a few hundred feet above the target asteroid's surface. Wearing spacesuits, the miners will emerge from the ship. Tiny jets mounted on their backs will guide them gently to the surface. There, they will hammer in spikes, attach long tethers to the spikes, and hook the ends of the tethers to their suits. This will keep them from accidentally floating away into space while they are working.

Living in Space

If the mining operation is scheduled to last a long time, engineers will build a habitat for the workers to live in. The building materials will be

NASA astronaut Shannon Lucid learns how to live in space, as asteroid miners will someday.

"cooked" out of the asteroidal rocks using a **solar oven**. Such an oven consists of large, lightweight mirrors that concentrate the sun's rays into one spot. The temperature at that spot will exceed 2,900 degrees Fahrenheit.

The solar oven can also process many of the mined materials. Mining methods will vary

An astronaut uses tiny jets to move through space.

according to the situation. For example, the dirt on the asteroid's surface may contain millions of small grains of various metals. The miners can separate and collect these grains using magnetic rakes. Larger deposits of metals and minerals will be separated with metal grinding and chopping machines. The loose materials will be nearly weightless, of course, so they will float up and away from the surface. But the miners will catch them in a large nylon canopy, or bag, that will surround the work area. Later, they will tie up the ends of the bag and tow it behind the ship back to Earth. Eventually, space stations, satellites, and even structures on Earth itself will be constructed from materials gathered from asteroids.

4
The Threat of Asteroid Impacts

Scientific interest in NEAs is not limited to mining valuable minerals and metals. Astronomers are increasingly studying these asteroids because they pose a potential threat to Earth, especially those that cross Earth's orbit. Occasionally, Earth's or the moon's gravity pulls an asteroid dangerously close. The impact of even a small asteroid striking Earth's surface could devastate a city. And larger asteroid impacts could kill millions of people and animals.

Numerous Impacts in the Past

The question is not whether an asteroid could or might strike Earth. Such impact events have occurred many times in the past. After all, that is how Earth formed in the first place. The planet grew larger and larger over the course of millions of years as it drew in planetesimals and asteroids. These objects crashed down, repeatedly reshaping the young Earth's surface.

Asteroids struck the moon, too. The thousands of craters visible on its surface are the scars of that bombardment. The moon's craters have survived intact because the moon has no air and water to erode them (wear them down).

Many of the craters on the moon formed from asteroid impacts.

Because the Earth is larger than the moon, it has stronger gravity. And not surprisingly, it has been struck by asteroids much more often than the moon has. However, the effects of rain, wind, tides, volcanoes, and so forth have eroded and erased the vast majority of Earth's craters.

One of the few easily visible impact craters remaining on Earth's surface lies near Winslow, Arizona. Known as Barringer Crater (or Meteor Crater), it is about three-quarters of a mile wide and some six hundred feet deep. It formed about twenty-five thousand years ago. An asteroid about one hundred feet across, weighing about sixty-three thousand tons, and traveling more than five miles per second smashed into the desert. The explosion created by the impact was enormous. It was several times larger than the one unleashed by the atomic bomb dropped on Hiroshima, Japan, at the end of World War II. Luckily, no people were killed because no one

Barringer Crater, in Arizona, is the telltale sign of a small asteroid colliding with Earth.

An artist captures the monstrous impact (left) of the asteroid that killed the dinosaurs (below).

lived in Arizona at the time.

By contrast, the dinosaurs were not so lucky. About 65 million years ago, long before the disaster that created Barringer Crater, a far larger asteroid collided with Earth. It was about six or so miles in diameter. The object struck the ocean near the eastern coast of Mexico with devastating force. It blasted out a crater more than one hundred miles across and several miles deep. This caused giant sea waves and huge earthquakes. The explosion also threw millions of tons of ash and dust into the atmosphere. The debris blocked sunlight for many months, making Earth's surface very dark and cold. The catastrophe wiped out about 70 percent of all the animal and plant species on the planet. Among the casualties were the dinosaurs, which had ruled Earth for more than 160 million years.

The Earth Is Still a Target

These disasters happened long ago. But Earth is still wide open to strikes by NEAs that occasionally stray too close. In 1908, an asteroid about the same size as the one that created Barringer Crater exploded over Tunguska, a remote region of Siberia (in eastern Russia). The area was largely uninhabited, so few people were killed. But the forests were completely flattened for a distance of almost twenty miles from ground zero. If the asteroid had struck only a few hours later, it would have wiped out St. Petersburg, Russia's second largest city.

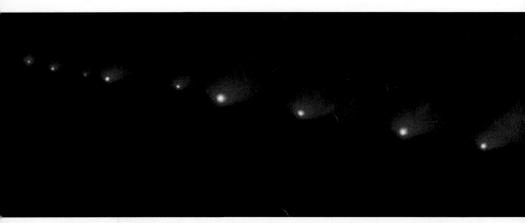

Pieces of Comet Shoemaker-Levy, which slammed into Jupiter's atmosphere in July 1994.

The destruction of a city would be terrible, of course. But at least most of humanity would survive. It is natural to ask if a much larger asteroid strike, like the one that killed the dinosaurs, could happen in the near future. Unfortunately, the answer is yes. In fact, people all over the world witnessed a series of such giant impacts in 1994. Between July 16 and July 22, twenty-one fragments of a large comet (an object similar to an asteroid) struck the planet Jupiter. Each fragment was a little over a mile across and blasted a hole the size of Earth in Jupiter's upper atmosphere. If this same series of objects had struck Earth, they would have killed every animal and human being on the planet.

Can Asteroid Impacts Be Prevented?

The solar system remains a dangerous place. All astronomers agree that sooner or later an NEA a mile or more in diameter will strike Earth. Hundreds of NEAs have been sighted and cataloged, and many thousands more are waiting to be found. Near encounters with the planets cause NEAs' orbits to change constantly. Some move farther away from Earth. But some move closer. And from time to time, one is bound to end up right in the planet's path.

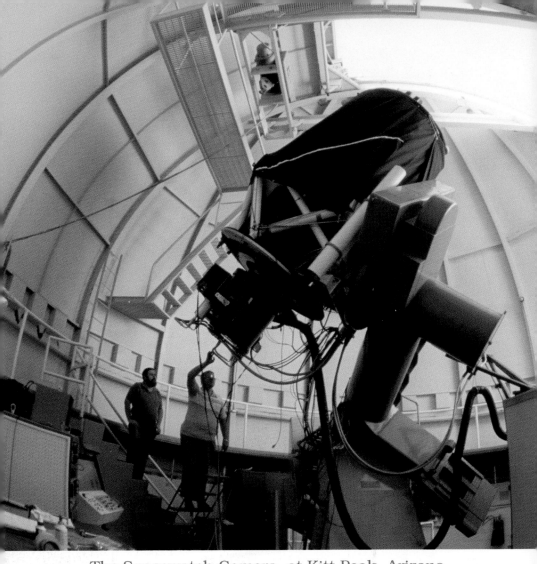

The Spacewatch Camera, at Kitt Peak, Arizona, searches for threatening asteroids.

The important question is what can people do to guard against asteroid impacts? First, scientists must locate and track NEAs and determine which ones might hit Earth. Scientists are doing this now. In the 1990s, the Spacewatch Camera went into operation at Kitt Peak, Arizona. It finds hundreds of new asteroids each year, about thirty of them NEAs. Also in the 1990s, a system called Near-Earth Asteroid Tracking (NEAT) opened on the summit of Mt. Haleakala, on Maui, Hawaii. (NEAT is co-sponsored by NASA and the U.S. Air Force.) In its first day of operation, it discovered four earth crossers; and it finds up to fifty earth crossers a month. Similar tracking systems are under construction in Europe.

Once scientists find an NEA on a collision course with Earth, the next step is to attempt to prevent a disastrous impact. Several popular movies about such impacts have depicted people using nuclear bombs to blow up an incoming

A scene from *Armageddon*, one of several films about an asteroid threatening Earth.

asteroid. In most cases, however, this approach is risky. Smashing the asteroid will usually produce numerous fragments, most of which will still be on a collision course with Earth. A hundred smaller impacts spread out over the planet's surface could be even more lethal than one large impact.

It would be better, many experts say, to nudge an incoming asteroid into a different orbit. That way it would miss Earth entirely. This might be done by exploding a nuclear bomb a few thousand feet from the object's surface. The force of the blast would not be enough to blow it up, but it *would* be enough to push it off course.

No one knows when such drastic steps will have to be taken. It could be fifty, a hundred, or five hundred years from now. Or it could be next month. One thing is certain. The more scientists learn about asteroids and other objects in the solar system, the better the chance humanity has of finding a way to survive in a hostile universe.

Glossary

asteroid: "Starlike object"; a small stony or metallic body orbiting the sun, most often in the asteroid belt.

asteroid belt: A region lying between the orbits of the planets Mars and Jupiter where most of the asteroids are located.

Bode's Law: A mathematical pattern recognized by Johann Bode, a German astronomer, in the nineteenth century. He pointed out that, moving outward from the sun, each known planet orbited at roughly twice the distance as the one before it.

compound asteroid: An asteroid consisting of two smaller asteroids held together by their mutual gravities.

gravity: A force exerted by an object that attracts

other objects. The pull of Earth's gravity keeps rocks, trees, people, and houses from floating away into space. It also holds the moon in its orbit around Earth.

impact crater: A hole in the ground created by the crash of an asteroid or other object from space.

mass: The total amount of matter contained in an object.

orbit: To move around something, or the path taken by a planet or other heavenly body around the sun (or a moon around a planet).

planet: A large solid or gaseous object orbiting the sun or another star.

planetesimals: Small objects that orbited the sun long ago and combined to form the planets.

process: To treat or prepare something to make it easier to use, or to separate a mixture into its individual parts.

solar oven: A device that uses mirrors to concentrate the sun's rays into one small area, producing a great deal of heat.

solar system: The sun and all of the objects that orbit it.

spherical: Round like a ball.

For Further Exploration

Mary A. Barnes and Kathleen Duey, *The Ultimate Asteroid Book: The Inside Story on the Threat from the Skies.* New York: Aladdin Paperbacks, 1998. An excellent introduction to asteroids and how they pose a potential threat to Earth.

Pam Beasant, *1000 Facts About Space.* New York: Kingfisher Books, 1992. An informative collection of basic facts about the stars, planets, asteroids, and other heavenly bodies.

Samantha Bonar, *Asteroids.* Danbury, CT: Franklin Watts, 2000. A general introduction to asteroids, highlighted by numerous photos.

Nigel Henbest, *DK Space Encyclopedia.* London: Dorling Kindersley, 1999. This beautifully mounted and critically acclaimed book is the best general source available for grade school readers about the wonders of space.

Douglas Henderson, *Asteroid Impact.* New York: Dial Books, 2000. A very handsomely illustrated volume that also contains much useful information about asteroids and how some of them have struck Earth.

Robin Kerrod, *The Children's Space Atlas: A Voyage of Discovery for Young Astronauts.* Brookfield, CT: Millbrook Press, 1992. A well-written, informative explanation of the stars, planets, comets, asteroids, and other objects making up the universe.

Gregory L. Vogt, *Asteroids, Comets, and Meteors.* Brookfield, CT: Millbrook Press, 1996. Tells the basic facts about these stony, metallic, and/or icy bodies orbiting the sun.

Index